ORANGUTANS

MONKEY DISCOVERY LIBRARY

Lynn M. Stone

Rourke Corporation, Inc.
Vero Beach, Florida 32964

PHOTO CREDITS

All photos © Lynn M. Stone

ACKNOWLEDGEMENTS

The author thanks the following for photographic assistance:
Lowry Park Zoological Garden, Tampa, Fla.; The Chester Zoo,
Chester, England

LIBRARY OF CONGRESS
Library of Congress Cataloging-in-Publication Data
Stone, Lynn M.
  Orangutans / by Lynn M. Stone.

  p. cm. — (Monkey discovery library)
  Summary: Describes the habitat, lifestyle, infancy, predators,
relationship with humans, and future of this great ape.
  ISBN 0-86593-065-1
  1. Orangutan—Juvenile literature. [1. Orangutans.] I. Title.
II. Series: Stone, Lynn M. Monkey discovery library.
QL737.P96S776   1990
599.88'44—dc20   90-32485
                                        CIP
                                        AC

TABLE OF CONTENTS

The Orangutan   5
The Orangutan's Cousins   6
How They Look   9
Where They Live   11
How They Live   14
The Orangutan's Babies   16
Predator and Prey   19
The Orangutan and People   20
The Orangutan's Future   22
Glossary   23
Index   24

ORANGUTANS

They are the closest of cousins, but a chimpanzee would never invite an orangutan to a party.

Of course, chimpanzees don't throw parties. But if they did, orangutans *(Pongo pygmaeus)* would never be on the guest list.

Like chimps, orangutans are great apes—giant sized monkeys. And orangs are big-brained, intelligent animals, just as chimps are.

But orangutans aren't nearly as loud and "friendly" as chimpanzees. Many orangs live alone.

For the shy orangutan, a good time is a tree full of ripe figs.

Orangutan

THE ORANGUTAN'S COUSINS

Along with chimpanzees, gorillas are also close cousins of orangutans. People are distant cousins of these great apes. Scientists are not sure which of the apes is most like us.

Like people, the great apes have no tail. They have forward facing eyes and fingers and toes which are similar to ours.

The apes have much longer and stronger arms than humans. An orangutan's arms dangle to its ankles. The arms of a big orangutan spread eight feet across!

Chimpanzee

HOW THEY LOOK

The orangutan has shaggy, reddish-brown hair. It is the "red" ape.

With stringy hair and sad eyes, an orang looks like it just climbed out of bed.

Orangs are about 46 to 55 inches long. A large male measured 60 inches.

Female orangs weigh from 65 to 110 pounds. Males weigh up to 200 pounds.

Adult orangs, especially males, have broad pads of fat around their faces.

Orangs have long, grasping fingers and toes. They can hold food with their toes.

9

WHERE THEY LIVE

Orangutans live on two large islands—Sumatra and Borneo—in Southeast Asia.

Sumatra is owned by Indonesia. Nearby is Borneo. Part of Borneo is owned by Indonesia. The rest is owned by Malaysia.

Most orangutans live in warm, wet forests called rain forests. This is their home, or **habitat.**

Orangs live in other types of forests as well. Some of them live in mountain forests 4800 feet above the lowland orangutans.

In the Malay language, orangutan means "man of the forest."

Orangutan

Young orangutan

Young orangutan

HOW THEY LIVE

Orangs spend most of their lives in trees. Scientists call animals of the trees **arboreal.**

Orangutans are the largest arboreal animals on earth. They are wonderful climbers, but swinging from tree to tree has risks.

Even with toes that work like fingers, many orangs break bones in falls. Orangutan bones, however, heal more quickly than human bones.

Orangs travel alone or in small groups. Most males live alone. Females are almost always with a baby.

Orangutans spend about four and one-half hours each day eating. At night they sleep in tree nests of branches.

THE ORANGUTAN'S BABIES

Baby orangutans learn how to be orangutans from their mothers. The "lessons" take five or six years. Only then does a young orangutan go off into the jungle on its own.

During its first year, the baby clings to its mother's underside. That allows the mother to use all her limbs in swinging through the trees.

Orangs in captivity have lived to be nearly 60.

Orangutan with baby

PREDATOR AND PREY

A **predator** is an animal which hunts other animals. The orangutan hunts only insects and eggs.

Orangutans are plant eaters, or **herbivores.** They eat fruit, bark, leaves, and flowers. They are especially fond of wild figs. As different kinds of figs ripen, orangutans move through the forest to stay with the ripe figs.

Large orangutans are not food, or **prey,** for predators. Baby orangs, however, are sometimes eaten by **pythons** and wild pigs.

Orangutan

THE ORANGUTAN AND PEOPLE

For hundreds of years, orangs were shot and trapped. Many females were killed so that their babies could be taken and sold to zoos.

The shooting and selling of wild orangs is no longer a big problem. Most people now are concerned about the future of these animals.

People studying orangs have shown that they can learn sign language just as chimps and gorillas have.

Orangs amuse and amaze people. One captive learned to open his cage door each night with a wire "key."

Young orangutan

THE ORANGUTAN'S FUTURE

Orangutans are **endangered** animals. They are in danger of some day disappearing forever.

Despite people's interest in these great apes, orangutan habitat is being destroyed.

As human numbers grow in Southeast Asia, there is a need for more farms and villages. Rain forest is being cut and burned.

By the 21st century, the wild "red" ape may survive only in the national parks of Sumatra and Borneo. Hopefully, Malaysia and Indonesia will save more of their island jungles for orangutans.

Glossary

arboreal (are BORE ee al)—living in trees

endangered (en DANE jerd)—in danger of no longer existing; very rare

habitat (HAB a tat)—the kind of place in which an animal lives, such as rain forest

herbivore (ERB a vore)—an animal which eats plants

predator (PRED a tor)—an animal that kills other animals for food

prey (PRAY)—an animal that is hunted by another for food

python (PIE thon)—a large snake that lives in several warm countries

INDEX

age 16, 20

apes 5, 6

arms 6, 16

babies 14, 16, 20

bones 14

chimpanzee 5, 20

color 9

eyes 6, 9

face 9

finger 6, 9, 14

food 5, 19

gorillas 6,20

habitat 112

hair 9

language 20

length 9

monkeys 5

people 6,20,22

predators 19

tail 6

toes 6,9

weight 9